THE CONFETTI PATH

101 Ways to Celebrate Your Passions and Inspire Creativity

GILAT BEN-DOR

GILAT
BEN-DOR
MEDIA, LLC

A
GUSTO POWER™
Book

GILAT
BEN-DOR
MEDIA, LLC

Published by Gilat Ben-Dor Media, LLC
6501 E. Greenway Pkwy., Suite 103
PMB 519
Scottsdale, AZ 85254
USA
http://GilatMedia.com

Cover design and interior layout by Gilat Ben-Dor.

For information or special discounts on bulk purchases, please contact Gilat Ben-Dor Media, LLC at address above, or
email: info@GilatMedia.com

ISBN-13: 978-0-9832674-0-9
ISBN-10: 0-983267-40-5

First printed in 2011

10 9 8 7 6 5 4 3 2 1

Printed in the U.S.A.

THE CONFETTI PATH

101 Ways to Celebrate Your Passions and Inspire Creativity

GILAT BEN-DOR

*With love and
gratitude to
my amazing
family*

*Mom, Dad,
Tami and
Orli*

*In memory of
Safta and
Saba*

*And to "The
Fortress"*

ADDITIONAL TITLES
BY GILAT BEN-DOR

The Rainbow Blueprint: An Action Journal for Those
with Many Passions

The GUSTO POWER® Workbook: Tactics and
Strategies for the Multi-Passionate Professional™

♦♦♦♦♦

For a complete list of Gilat Ben-Dor's publications since the
last printing of this book, please visit http://GilatMedia.com

THE CONFETTI PATH
Contents

Introduction

I n Milos Forman's 1984 film, *Amadeus*, based on the life of classical composer Mozart, there is a scene I will never forget. Austrian emperor Joseph II complained to Mozart that his latest masterpiece had "too many notes." When the emperor suggested that Mozart "just cut a few, and it'll be perfect," Mozart was outraged. He indignantly responded, "Which *few* did you have in mind, Majesty?"

This example reminds me of the situations in which many creative spirits often find themselves. From family members and partners to work colleagues and bosses, there is a frustrated complaint that their creative friend/partner/child/employee is playing with "too many notes," so to speak. They should just figure out what it is they want to do, and just do it!

This seems to be the common outcry from those on a more conventional path, those who do not realize that the exploration itself is the point; that the variety and sampling is not always a sign of confusion or a woeful lack of focus. This "buffet of being" is, in fact, a deliberate and highly engaging way of savoring life for a certain type of individual.

As an intensely creative spirit myself, I have been bucking against this often unspoken expectation (that is, to "pick the

One Thing") for years. But even in my staunch rebellion of it, I have continued to feel its presence: in colleges, in families, in the job market, and even in institutions where young children are influenced. Without a doubt, there is a widespread societal pressure to "pick one thing and stick with it," to celebrate the single-minded specialist as one who has achieved success by way of laser-sharp focus, and to equate that solitary path with the only road to respectable accomplishment.

Yet, one size does not fit all. If passion and perseverance breed success (and what is the true meaning of success, anyway?) then do those who reluctantly sacrifice all but one passion truly position themselves for success and fulfillment? Is there any credit for self-denial (and if so, *why*)? For the multi-passionate, creative spirit, success lies more in the journey, the many flavors along the way; the kernel of joy lies in the freedom to simulta-neously explore the intriguing paths and passions of this lifetime.

I wrote THE CONFETTI PATH as a way of honoring all of the multi-talented, multi-passionate individuals whose natural curiosity and creativity are a gift to be celebrated.

These days, with information, technology and other resources so readily available (and relatively inexpensive), exploring a new interest or indulging in a passion no longer has to mean a hefty investment of time or money. It's time to take the apologetic nature out of wanting to sample and explore a range of activities and directions, and get to the business of doing so proudly, and living authentically to the max.

Of course, for those who prefer to go "all in" in one area, kudos to you; there is no one superior approach to anything, as long as it feels true to your spirit. But if you do want to fit in a wide spectrum of passions into one lifetime, especially simultaneously, the "sampling" strategy may be more suitable and efficient for your purposes.

As you read the pages of THE CONFETTI PATH, ask yourself: What are some rituals or activities I can easily add into my life—or even try out once with no pressure to "commit?"

THE CONFETTI PATH seeks to celebrate *you*—the individual who has not one, nor two, nor even three burning passions, but many more. Embrace your appetite for life's spectrum of flavors in the course of daily living, and nourish your unquenchable curiosity for life's colorful components.

Amid the pages of THE CONFETTI PATH, the close link between passion and creativity is allowed to unfold in full bloom, so that one fuels the other: enjoying passions fuels the joy and energy that allow creative ideas to flow freely, while using heightened creativity to further enhance the way you express and explore your passions.

May THE CONFETTI PATH help you to unleash the freedom of expression and joyful, never-a-dull-moment style of living that will bring you true fulfillment along your colorful path. By virtue of us being alive, able-bodied, and thirsting for activity, we are well-equipped to live life as a genuine celebration.

Gilat Ben-Dor
Scottsdale, Arizona

People and Community

"Call it a clan, call it a network, call it a tribe, call it a family: Whatever you call it, whoever you are, you need one."

-Jane Howard

1

Join special-interest groups.

Seek out special-interest groups to match your range of passions. There are some great websites that help centralize various groups' activities by interest and by city, such as MeetUp.com. From foreign language practice to travel buffs, to Law of Attraction and Entrepreneur Moms, there is something for everyone. Or else start your own group!

2

Engage in non-annoying networking.

In some circles, the term "networking" has gotten a bad rap, either for being boring or done in a soulless, going-through-the-motions manner in hopes of gaining business leads. When done in the spirit of sharing and truly taking an interest in the people around you, you can learn a great deal about others and experience some impromptu conversations that may lead to more opportunities on your path.

3

Choose your partner well.

Whether your business partner or your life partner (or even a travel partner), matching personalities, lifestyles, and key passions can complement your own endeavors. Even if you do not share all the same interests, a partner should be supportive of your passions and visions, and nurturing to your creative spirit. And vice versa.

4

Volunteer your time and spirit.

Time and talents, when directed in the service of others, is time well-spent. By the sharing of yourself to help those less fortunate, or to help a charitable cause you believe in, you expand your energy into the rewarding realms of love, joy, and caring—key channels that lead to abundance and creativity.

5

Diversify your friendships.

When you branch out into varied groups of friends, each group can speak to a different side of you, creating a social web that is customized just to you. For example, your photography friends, your church friends, your animal activist friends, and your investment club friends may never meet each other, but they all connect through the unique being that is you, and add a social spark to the expression of each passion.

6

Shooting the breeze is also important.

Remember to carve out regular meetings with friends for coffee, lunch or other purely social events. This is a particularly valuable practice if you are often plagued by stress and feel overwhelmed about projects and deadlines.

Taking brief but regular periods to stay connected with true friends will help you to recharge, and to avoid the burn-out or pressure to "be productive" every single moment of the day. Like a glossy magazine spread, it is often the "white space" in our days that helps bring the other pieces into context.

7

Do not be a slave to "social media."

Whether for business or personal activities, the social media (a.k.a., social networking) trend has taken our plugged-in society by storm. While there are ways to complement our passions by connecting with like-minded people and groups through sites like Facebook.com and LinkedIn.com, it is important to keep the constant updates and responses from becoming an addiction. If you enjoy social media, think about a strategy that will benefit you, your passions, and your goals, and use it as one tool to get you there.

8

Choose your role models and study them.

Read the biographies of people you admire, and learn about their unique paths to success. What about them do you respect? How did they get to where they are today? What obstacles did they overcome, and how? If you look up to someone you know personally, ask them if they would be your mentor and offer you periodic guidance over a lunch meeting (your treat!).

9

Host a dinner party and invite an unlikely mix of people.

I am told that Before World War II, my great-grandfather managed the Budapest Opera House. He was known for hosting many spirited gatherings at his home involving artists, musicians, patrons, writers, philosophers, and other cultural luminaries of the time. What an evening it must have been every time!

Who among your own circle would blend in interesting ways? Bring together a diverse mix of people from different parts of your life. New ideas and lively conversations do wonders for sparking the creative muse, long after the last guest has gone home.

10

Speak your heart out.

Do you enjoy public speaking? Maximize the exhilaration of connecting with an audience, sharing your message, and creating more opportunities to showcase your talents and passions. Why choose among your passions? Create a quality speech about each area of your interests, and see where it takes you! There are several organizations, like the National Speakers Association (nsaspeaker.org) and Toastmasters (toastmasters.org) that can help get you started.

11

Benefit from animal magnetism.

Animals provide a powerful gateway to love, and even stress relief. Those conditions support an atmosphere of letting our hair down and feeling confident to explore and create. Adopt a pet from a local shelter. When treated with love and respect, animals reciprocate with unconditional devotion, affection, and pure positive energy from within. This spirit of comfort and support adds to an ideal environment for creativity.

CONFETTI REFLECTION

When it comes to **people and community,** what are some unique ways that you express your passions and creativity? What new ideas can you explore in this area? Use the spaces below to jot down your thoughts.

1._____

_____

2._____

_____

3._____

_____

4._____

_____

5._____

_____

Education and Events

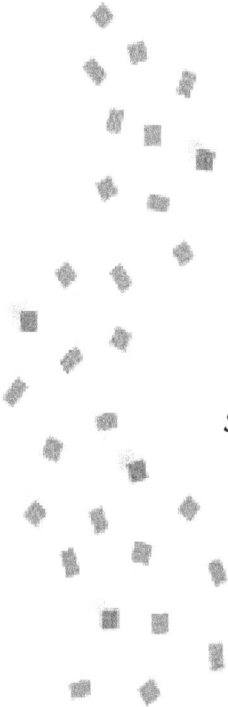

"Learn something new. Try something different. Convince yourself that you have no limits."

-Brian Tracy

12

Be credible while being incredible.

Take your passions to the next level by obtaining certifications or other recognized credentials in those fields. Whether or not you are currently working in your areas of passion, building expertise in these areas will prepare you for any paths you may want to take later. No learning is ever wasted!

13

Lifelong Learning + Camaraderie =

Great Things.

Expand on your interests both broadly and specifically. Drill down or get an overview of your passions through seminars, workshops, and other forms of continuing education.

These are generally faster (and less costly) than going for a full college degree in these areas, but they provide you with current information on trends, strategies and techniques in a focused way. Best of all, if you choose the live formats of these events (as opposed to online or self-paced formats) you will easily meet others who are like-minded…adding to the momentum of your explorations.

14

Explore the Expo's.

Being surrounded by tens of thousands of square feet of booths, materials, people, and demonstrations about a single topic can be thrilling. For a hands-on experience on the front lines of your passion—the more specific, the better—attend a trade show or expo, and immerse yourself in another world. Remember to bring a big bag for "swag" (give-away goodies).

15

Your newspaper is a rich educational resource.

Check your local paper for the calendar section. There are often numerous lectures and other educational events advertised and held at the city library and other accessible venues. Don't limit yourself to a particular topic area; if something different sounds intriguing, follow your instincts and check it out.

16

Tap into university life.

Do you live in a college town? Most larger towns and cities have at least one university, which typically offers a wealth of events, from lectures and symposia with distinguished speakers, to poetry readings, and historical renditions of plays and performances. Sometimes, just being back on a college campus can reignite the thirst for knowledge, and the will to do something big with it!

17

Sponsor your own lecture series.

If the combination of leadership, program design, and event planning (and promotion) appeals to you, consider starting your own lecture series. Decide on a unifying theme, the duration of your series (for example, once a month for 6 months), and the venue, which can rotate at different homes if the series is created privately among friends.

Decide if you will charge for the series and whether you will hire professional (paid) speakers or not, and how you will promote the event. The first series may feel a bit bumpy but who knows—this could be a great way to showcase your own range of talents!

CONFETTI REFLECTION

When it comes to **education and events,** what are some unique ways that you express your passions and creativity? What new ideas can you explore in this area? Use the spaces below to jot down your thoughts.

1._____

_____

2._____

_____

3._____

_____

4._____

_____

5._____

_____

Reading and Writing

"Reading, like writing, is a creative act. If readers only bring a narrow range of themselves to the book, then they'll only see their narrow range reflected in it."

-Ben Okri

18

Keep a journal.

Keep a journal where you record thoughts, inspirations, and challenges in your life. You can look back at entries from the past to see how you have changed, or what sparked particular inspirations. Documenting aspects of your life, large or small, can also sharpen your observations, which in turn enhance your natural creativity. For added inspiration, treat yourself to the most beautiful journal you can find.

19

Gather up your favorite blogs.

Blogs may range in quality and professionalism, but the right blog can pull you into the blogger's world and immerse you in their microcosm of thoughts, opinions, photos, links, and even contests, a dynamic micro-publication all about your passions. Hunt for blogs about a range of your interests, and create a custom directory of them for easy reference.

20

Be the blogger.

We are living in exciting times. Anyone with a passion can create their own, original blog. You decide the theme(s). You decide how often to post, and what you will post about. Will you allow guest bloggers? Will you include special features like video series and product reviews? If you prefer not to deal with the technical aspects of setting up a blog, you can obtain a free and instant blog at websites like Wordpress.com and Blogger.com. Or get ahead of the curve with the fast-growing Tumblr.com.

21

Be a Comment Commando.

If starting your own blog is not your cup of tea, post your thoughts as comments to existing blogs. There are entire subcultures around the "regulars" who contribute their thoughts, ideas, and sometimes, strong reactions, to the blogs they follow. Visit blog directories like Technorati.com to discover some of the latest and hottest blogs in the "blogosphere" right now.

22

Give yourself the Bookstore Test.

Lose yourself amid the shelves of a bookstore, and see which topics attract you most that day. I have used this exercise for my coaching clients who struggle to discover what their passions are. This is a great way to see where the creative muse is taking you at a given point in time. Explore your findings further.

23

Brainstorm your book title.

Have you wanted to write your own book? Nothing gets the creative juices pumping, and the inspiration jumping, better than brainstorming the title of your own book or book series. Will it be a novel? A non-fiction volume? A mini gift book? What are you already an expert on, that you also love to talk about?

24

Picture your own book cover.

Besides brainstorming a title, this is another way to get the creative juices flowing when envisioning your book. If you are artistically or technically inclined, create sketches or digital samples of the cover of your book. Good, old-fashioned colored pencils, markers, and paper work wonderfully, too. You can create several different versions, and survey friends about them, if you feel comfortable. As with any goal in your mind, start to see your book as a tangible reality.

25

Read niche magazines.

It's exciting to discover a publication that caters to that niche passion you've always loved. Wow! A whole magazine—just for that? Jackpot! Browse larger bookstores and airport news shops to find an array of hard-to-find and niche publications. Search online for additional options for industry trade publications. Buy one or subscribe, for something to look forward to in your mailbox.

26

Freelance your passion.

Put your pen (or keyboard) to work! See if your favorite trade journals or association newsletters accept outside submissions, and contribute your best articles about a timely, related topic. This is another way to build your "passion creds" when branching out within your desired fields.

27

Form a book club.

Go beyond the best-seller list. Join or form a themed book club based on a specialized passion, such as politics, gardening, cooking, or crime novels. You can even initiate an unusual theme such as books by foreign authors or books that all take place in the same region—your home state, for example.

28

Join a writer's group.

Join an existing writer's group or form your own to share the writing experience with others, and gain valuable feedback. Just as book clubs have themes, join or create a group that will have a focus. It could be a group based on novel writing, non-fiction, poetry—or a theme based not on the type of writing, but on the attendees: a women's group or some other common denominator among the writers.

29

Write a letter—by hand.

Remember the lost art of letter-writing? The pen is still mighty. Write a letter to someone special, or as a way to heal from past hurts and release blocks that may have been hindering your creativity. Choose to send it or not. For the feeling of Old World indulgence, purchase the finest writing papers you can find, and use a fountain pen.

CONFETTI REFLECTION

When it comes to **reading and writing,** what are some unique ways that you express your passions and creativity? What new ideas can you explore in this area? Use the spaces below to jot down your thoughts.

1._____

_____

2._____

_____

3._____

_____

4._____

_____

5._____

_____

Passion and Business

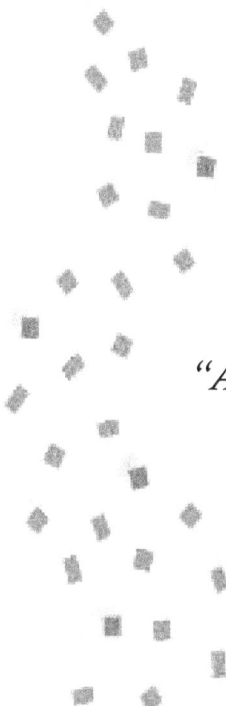

"All the things I love is what my business is all about."

\- Martha Stewart

30

Start a business customized

to your passions.

For many creative souls, having their own business is not only a road to autonomy and freedom, but a business can be a form of creative expression in itself. Whether home-based or on-site, or even as a part-time side business, use this avenue as a profitable way to combine multiple passions—in unusual ways!

For instance, someone who loves dogs and painting can create a business selling their dog-themed paintings and prints online or through a gallery. Do you love science and children? You could form a science tutoring business for kids, or write a fun book for teenagers about how the world works from a scientific point of view. The possibilities are virtually limitless!

31

Form a mastermind group.

The well-known saying, "Two heads are better than one," has been popular for a reason. Gathering regularly with a group of supportive, motivated individuals—whether 5 or 15—and strategizing about each person's individual goals can yield tremendous creative capital. The ideas, tactics and insights that are generated through the group's collective experiences and knowledge are often much greater than the brainstorming of one person alone.

32

Speak often, and publicly,

about your passion.

Yes, this is another tip about public speaking, but this time, think of your talk as a business strategy. Some people go into professional speaking because they simply love to speak. Others find themselves speaking publicly because of their passion for their topic. Whichever started first, the two often blend, as you create interesting talks about your beloved topics, and you become connected with your audiences. Even if speaking is not your main focus, it can also be used as a marketing tool for that creative business you've formed!

33

Coach or consult in the areas you love.

Who better than to become well-versed on all of the trends, challenges and solutions of an industry than the person who is passionate about the field? Another way to incorporate your passions in business is to become a consultant—a solution provider to your clients, or a coach—a supportive facilitator of your client's own empowerment.

If you are passionate about building relationships and maintaining your network, you might consider becoming a communications coach; if you are fascinated with stained glass, and you know all about preserving it, you might consult for religious or historic preservation organizations. Just be sure that you are following any legal and industry regulations before hanging your shingle.

34

There is a professional association for just about everything.

My sisters used to tease me because I have belonged to just about every type of association out there. That's a good thing! From cake decorating to management consulting, there is a professional association, club, alliance, consortium or other organizational body for just about any interest, hobby, or professional predilection out there.

Search online with terms like "[name of passion] association" and you should soon find a number of groups in your field. Many of these associations are nationally or internationally based, and are composed of local chapters throughout the country. Check for one near you.

35

Attend industry conferences

in your desired field.

This tip does not emphasize merely attending conferences in your current field. That may be a good idea if you are fortunate to be working in an area of your passion already. But you need not stick to an area you have "fallen into" if it is not your calling. Why not try out a conference about another passion you've been meaning to explore?

Just like trade shows, you can immerse yourself in an insulated world of people, ideas and tools that matter to your heart. And unlike trade shows, conferences tend to last for even longer and emphasize ongoing programs of speakers and workshops. If you are lucky enough to find a trade show/conference combination about your favorite topic, jump on it!

36

Be a conference presenter.

I have already suggested speaking publicly about your passions, but going to conferences as a presenter takes this to an entirely different level. You may be traveling far from home, and this circumstance alone tends to open up the spirit of adventure. Speaking at a conference, even if in a smaller break-out session, will put you on the radar as an expert in your chosen topic area. And with that, the gates of creativity, passion, and confidence will swing right open!

37

Collect quotes that truly move you.

When was the last time you came across an inspirational quote that *truly* moved you – that made you stop and say, "Wow – that's a good one!" Just because a quote is famous does not mean it inspires you personally. Collect only those quotes that truly resonate with you, and display them in places you'd like to be reminded of them. Perhaps in your office or work studio, or keep a print-out of your favorites in your car for a boost of insight on your way to your important events.

CONFETTI REFLECTION

When it comes to **passion and business,** what are some unique ways that you express this passion and creativity? What new ideas can you explore in this area? Use the spaces below to jot down your thoughts.

1._____

_____

2._____

_____

3._____

_____

4._____

_____

5._____

_____

Creativity and Motivation

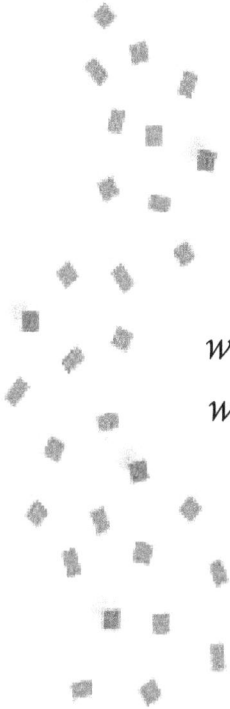

"Do not wait; the time will never be "just right." Start where you stand, and work with whatever tools you may have at your command, and better tools will be found as you go along."

-Napoleon Hill

38

Capture your ideas when you can.

Few things are more frustrating than having a brilliant idea—in the shower, while driving, or lying in bed—and not reaching a pen and paper fast enough to record them. While there may be some delay necessary to, say, grab a towel, give yourself frequent opportunities to jot down your flashes of insight. Keep multiple sets of pens and papers handy, by your bed, on your desk, in your purse or briefcase, and yes—in your car. You never know when your Next Great Idea will strike.

39

Organize your work area

the way *you* like it.

If you like a light and airy space, full of sunshine in the daytime, make it happen. If you feel cramped and annoyed by a cluttered work environment, get yourself organized. Even if you need to make significant changes or move spaces, the effort will be worthwhile. Our physical and mental "spaces" are closely tied together. Reclaiming a desk, office, or studio and making it comfortable for your individual needs can profoundly affect the quality, and quantity, of your creative output.

40

Treat yourself to beautiful

instruments of your craft.

Just like a concert pianist demands the finest piano on which to play, and a race car driver requires top-notch specs on her vehicle, so should you seek out the most beautiful, functional, and high-quality instruments involved in your own vocation. Use the finest notebooks, pens, computers, clothing, corkscrews, or any other accoutrements you can afford. The payoff will be increased pride and satisfaction in what it is that you do.

41

Purchase (or create) artwork

that inspires you.

If we are wise, we pay careful attention to the company that we keep. We want to be selective with those who share our space and energy. In the same way, the objects in our familiar spaces should also add—and not detract—from our aesthetic experiences. There are times we must live or work in a space reflecting someone else's taste. But whenever possible, carve out your own expressive areas and fill them with objects, artwork, furniture, and lighting that paint a perfect picture of you.

42

Change the scenery.

Whether you work from home, from a cubicle, or anywhere else called work, be sure to take frequent breaks to recharge your mind. It is a known fact that performing mundane drudgery can be draining; but surprisingly, so can the mental efforts of inspired creative output. Take breaks, and mix things up during those breaks to give your mind a true hiatus. Move to a different location for a literal change of scenery—leave your desk and head outside, get a snack, call a friend, or watch a snippet of a favorite video. Your creative brain will thank you.

43

Explore your inner terrain while driving.

Driving, especially when alone in the car, can be a contempla-tive experience, a time to reflect. Depending on your mood, you may seek silence or prefer to listen to your favorite tunes. But for a change of pace, and an uplifting activity, find audio programs that intrigue you, and listen to them on your drive. From audio novels to motivational content, from business tips to relaxation tracks, you may find that your audio collection will soon grow—along with an appetite for listening on the road. Thanks to portable players and headphones, take your audio experience with you on the bus, train, or plane, too.

44

Take part in brain teasers.

Research findings in recent years have suggested that maintaining an active mind serves us well as we age. But at any age, taking a playful approach to mental workouts can help keep the spark alive when it comes to generating ideas and keeping the energy flowing through our minds.

Experiment with different games, whether played solo or with friends; online or on a board; with pen and paper, cards, or game pieces. Try Sudoku, word games, jigsaw puzzles, and the latest video game consoles. Some interactive console games even combine physical elements, like dance steps, into the mix.

45

Visit stores that pique your interest.

Browse stores for inspiration, ideas, or another way to unwind and give your mind some needed "white space." Lose yourself in a cozy bookstore, game shop, artist supply or crafts store, or even at the fashion mall. Buy if you're inspired to, but this exercise works just as well without making a single purchase. Instead, imagine ideal scenes relating to your discoveries. Where would you wear that beautiful red dress you just spotted? What would you paint with those pigments? To whom would you send those exquisite note cards?

46

Keep a giant, dry-erase board handy.

Think of yourself as the coach of a sports team, strategizing the game on a big chalkboard. But in this case, the team members are your collection of passions and talents, and the game is your life. There is hidden power in writing down your ideas and organizing your goals. The beauty of a dry-erase board is its flexible nature, always open for revisions. Keep your board in plain view, and use it to brainstorm or track your goal progress.

47

Get silly!

Sometimes we take ourselves sooo seriously. This is not fun. And more importantly, it doesn't help to fan the flames of pursuing our passions, or innovating cool stuff. First, realize when you need some loosening up (do a regular self-check on this). Then, whether alone or with a friend, do something silly.

Watch re-runs of comedy TV or go see the latest funny movie. Combine words in ridiculous ways (think of the "jeggings" trend—that questionable combination of jeans and leggings). Play "stand-up comic" and come up with the goofiest jokes, delivered aloud to your (possibly imaginary) audience. Chances are, you'll be the one laughing hardest!

CONFETTI REFLECTION

> When it comes to **creativity and motivation,** what are some unique ways that you express your passions and creativity? What new ideas can you explore in this area? Use the spaces below to jot down your thoughts.

1._____

_____

2._____

_____

3._____

_____

4._____

_____

5._____

_____

Travel and Discovery

"The real voyage of discovery consists not in seeking new landscapes but in having new eyes."

- Marcel Proust

48

Visit the land of your passions.

Seek out a destination that ties into your passion, and plan a vacation around it. Since I was twelve years old, I knew I had to visit Florence, Italy and explore my passion for Italian Renaissance art. Years later, I spent a semester living out this dream, and to this day, I think of that time often. Is there a place close to your heart that you've always wanted to visit and explore? Deciding where to go, planning the journey, and of course, savoring the adventure itself, can provide you years of creative capital and unforgettable memories.

49

Delight in the charms

of a botanical garden.

If your city has a botanical garden, take advantage of this beautiful oasis of the mind, body and spirit. Take a camera, a snack, and a journal and pen, and stroll among the delightful gardens and lush, winding paths. Look for birds or butterflies. You may even want to bring a sketch pad or some background music with headphones.

50

Go to the zoo.

There is something appealingly playful and wholesome about spending a day at the zoo. In modern society, zoo animals are well-treated in comfortable habitats, and it is fascinating to observe or interact with a wide range of beautiful, unusual creatures live and up close. Being around animals in a loving state of mind expands our empathy and compassion, opening gateways to more love—and consequently, more meaningful living.

51

Chat with the locals.

When traveling far from home, making connections in the community takes on a different energy. Talk with locals about your latest passions. When you are away from home, it is much easier—and more exciting—to reinvent yourself! New acquaintances do not know your past, and cannot pigeon-hole you for what you've become known for back home. This is a great time to test out your new ideas and present your updated identity.

52

Take a cross-country road trip.

If you have a car and can carve out some time, hit the road! With its big skies, endless stretches of highways, or (depending on your part of the world) scenic forests or shorelines, the open road has beckoned many a dreaming spirit. Classic films like *National Lampoon's Vacation* and *Thelma and Louise*, and legendary highways like America's Route 66 are evidence of the sense of adventure and introspection that a road trip brings.

53

Document your road adventures.

One of the most famous creative works resulting from a road trip was Jack Kerouac's 1957 novel, *On the Road*. If life is like a movie (or a novel), your road trip could be a juicy chapter, documented in grand detail through a journal, a camera, a sketch book, or even as a video journal. Be reflective and solitary, or interactive, interviewing or writing about the interesting characters that you meet along the way. After all, you are the writer, producer, director, *and* star of this production.

54

Exhibit your travel photos.

When you return from your travels, sift through your photos and compile a collection of your best. If you've written poems or vignettes with each photo, include those. Decide on the theme and a catchy title for your collection, and approach a local gallery or coffee house—or an open-minded travel agent or car dealership—with an offer of exhibiting your work as a draw for their clients. Remember to think outside the box: What other businesses might like to have a travel exhibit linked to their products or services?

55

Take a different route to work.

Travel and adventure are powerful ways to beckon our passion and stir our creative juices. But we can do this while staying close to home, too. If you drive to work, why not mix things up and take a different route to work? You may discover a new neighborhood, or shops and restaurants to revisit later. Either way, changing your route to work is a fun way to refresh your senses and overcome the stale feeling of going through the motions of the same old commute.

56

Get lost (on purpose).

Have you ever discovered something great by accident? You can easily recreate these conditions—by getting lost on purpose! When I lived abroad, I would sometimes take a train or a bus spontaneously, with no agenda, and get off at a stop that looked interesting. You can even do this in your own city. Notice the details of your new surroundings, and again, bring along a camera or a journal if you enjoy documenting your quest. Just make sure that you are venturing into safe areas (ask a trusted local before you disembark at an unknown neighborhood).

57

Visit a farmer's market.

The beauty and bounty of nature are deliciously evident at farmer's markets, which have sprouted up all over the globe. Show up with your shopping sack and a spontaneous spirit, and get ready to taste and to mingle. Sample the goodness of fresh produce and artisanal delicacies, and talk with the farmers and specialists that make it all happen. These simple pleasures bring us gratitude and joy, and help make life a real treat.

58

Go on a treasure hunt.

Browse flea markets, antique shops, and estate sales for hidden treasures and beautiful objects from bygone eras. A unique object has the power to stir the imagination and transport us to another time and place—a great state of mind for dreaming and creating.

CONFETTI REFLECTION

When it comes to **travel and discovery,** what are some unique ways that you express your passions and creativity? What new ideas can you explore in this area? Use the spaces below to jot down your thoughts.

1._____

_____

2._____

_____

3._____

_____

4._____

_____

5._____

Arts, Science and Culture

"Culture is the widening of the mind and of the spirit."

- Jawaharlal Nehru

59

Explore a museum.

Who says you have to travel far and wide to wander through a museum? Most cities and even smaller towns have at least one museum. From art museums to historical societies, you may have passed one by in your hometown without ever going in. Take an afternoon—or even an hour—and explore the rooms of these special institutions. Check to see if there are other events happening that day, such as a lecture, film, or special exhibit. Peek into the gift shop for unusual finds.

60

Attend a film festival.

Film festivals are an ideal way to experience a concentration of new films, often around a theme or by independent filmmakers. Whether artistic, foreign, or unique in their storylines, independently-produced films can provide a refreshing take to the movie experience. Even without a film festival, most cities have a movie theatre specializing in independent films, so get ready for yet another way to experience some drama.

61

Go to the symphony.

Classical music is a marvel. Just imagine: Before the luxuries of modern technology, most of the melodies were written by hand and each instrument's part was intricately orchestrated in the composer's mind, all without the aid of software, electronic playback, or multi-track simulation. To hear these stunning works live adds a breathtaking dimension to this feat of human imagination and creativity.

62

Indulge in the opera.

As if classical scores of music were not complex works in and of themselves, imagine these works put to lyrics, building on a lively storyline and a witty *libretto*. Next, add beautiful costumes, lush set design, and a talented cast of opera singers. And what is the result? One of the most exquisite examples of passion and creativity combined into a single production. Even if opera music is not your cup of tea, try attending at least one performance and notice the separate facets of the production all coming together masterfully.

63

Experience the ballet.

Just like the opera, a ballet is the culmination of several artistic media expertly combined for an extraordinary effect. The ballet offers us a refined sense of story and drama: Haunting melodies, performed with grace and gusto; ethereal set design and willowy costumes; and painstaking choreography paired flawlessly to the music—all brought to life by a celebrated cast of world-class dancers. The ballet infuses a timeless sense of grace and beauty into every measure played, every moment danced.

64

Discover jazz.

Jazz became an American musical style that took the world by storm. Based on the concepts of syncopation, improvisation, and other methods of vocal and instrumental creativity, jazz has come to represent musical freedom, innovation, and a colorful experience for both performer and listener alike.

65

Go see a play.

Whether famous like Shakespeare or up-and-coming, play-wrights and their theatre productions have inspired generations with their works. Social, political and cultural commentary spring forth from the stage, and vivid plots unfold in real time, taking the audience with them on their dramatic capers. How will a good play affect you? There is only one way to find out.

66

Be the voice of arts and culture.

Attending arts and cultural events puts you in direct contact with a world of passion, energy, and creative expression—a mix that is bound to rub off on like-minded souls. To feel even more connected to the scene, post reviews or short articles of the performances and exhibits that you attend. These can be posted on blogs or even submitted to the arts or citizen sections of some local publications.

67

Marvel at the wonders of science.

If you live near a science museum, take advantage of it. Child-like wonder ripens the creative flow even for adults, and this can be done while learning about the world around us in the form of cool, hands-on exhibits and fun facts. Some science centers or natural history museums will have a planetarium, too. Pop in for a show! When we see the magic in both big and little things in our physical world, the world of our mind expands, too.

68

Volunteer for the arts.

Combining a passion for the arts, for community, and for helping others is easy, by becoming a volunteer for the arts. Ask your favorite museum or organization how you can help. Consider becoming a museum docent, theatre usher, or a volunteer at your city's symphony hall. You could form memorable friendships through this activity, and you will also infuse your life with exciting cultural experiences.

69

Study about a foreign country.

Have you ever felt a particular pull towards a country, like you wanted to know everything about France, Japan, or Argentina? Some people feel inexplicably drawn to a particular country, even if they've never been there and have no family heritage from the place. Visiting would be ideal, but even from your own home you can experience a total immersion. Research the country's geography, learn about the culture, and discover the people's unique history, customs, and cuisine. It would not be a surprise if the universe sent some opportunities to travel there!

70

Learn a foreign language.

One way to immerse yourself in a culture that intrigues you is to study its language. Perhaps this language will come in handy in other ways, too. Foreign language classes are offered regularly at most community colleges and adult continuing education programs. Besides live classes, there are numerous ways to learn a new language through online forums, software, audio CDs, private tutoring, or by joining a foreign-language special interest group (see Tip #1).

71

Roam around an art supply store.

Even if you've never gone "pro" with your art, your inner artist deserves to be celebrated. Browse an art supply store and discover your preferred artistic medium. Treat yourself to some supplies and go to a calming space and experiment. Great ideas that begin in clay or canvas can spark ideas for completely different projects.

72

Sign up for art classes.

Survey the offerings of your local college or continuing education center. What interests you at the moment? Perhaps you've painted in the past, but now you'd like to try pottery. Or printmaking. Or mosaics. Or perhaps creative writing. What if you finally registered for that photography course you've been meaning to take? An added bonus for taking these classes: like-minded creative individuals are drawn together, and both new friendships and new ideas can blossom.

73

Meet an artist.

Visit a gallery opening, browse online artist websites, or find an artist studio open to the public, and arrange to meet the artist in person. One of the best ways to learn more about the expression of passion and creativity is to study the process, which can vary with each individual. Ask the artist about their own creative approaches, challenges, and triumphs. Can you apply parts of this to your own creative process?

74

Become a collector.

After visiting museums, and perusing art books, galleries and websites, or after years of cultural exposure, you may develop strong preferences for certain types of art. Start a collection of original artwork, sculpture and/or photography. Get to know the artist(s) personally, if possible. If your collection grows large enough, and the theme is intriguing, organize a local exhibit or loan your collection to a willing venue.

75

Go commercial with your art.

If you have an entrepreneurial spirit, translate your artwork into an online sales stream through Internet auction sites like eBay.com or through your own web-based gallery. Think big! While original artwork draws one type of market, there are many other markets for prints and other products upon which to imprint your artwork, from greeting cards to mouse pads, T-shirts to mugs. You can also look into licensing your images to others, from clothing companies to stock image providers.

76

Explore the avenue of music.

Are you musically inclined? It is never too late to learn—or resume playing—a musical instrument. Which instruments can you imagine yourself playing? Are you taken by Chopin's haunting nocturnes on the piano? Are you mesmerized by the soulful melodies of the violin? Perhaps your style is more in line with the jazzy saxophone, or the visceral beats of the drum. Seek out a local music instructor and treat yourself to some lessons. Soon, the world around you will seem rhythmic in surprising ways.

77

Compose your own works.

Do you catch yourself humming to an original tune, or scrawling song lyrics on the back of your junk mail envelopes? Utilize technology to translate your compositions into multi-instrument performances using electronic keyboards and other devices. If you want the potential for broad exposure for your works, research the market and submit your tracks to music marketplace websites like iTunes.com as a distribution option.

CONFETTI REFLECTION

When it comes to **arts, science and culture**, what are some unique ways that you express your passions and creativity? What new ideas can you explore in this area? Use the spaces below to jot down your thoughts.

1._____

_____

2._____

_____

3._____

_____

4._____

_____

5._____

Gourmet Pursuits

"Some people like to paint pictures, or do gardening, or build a boat in the basement.

Other people get a tremendous pleasure out of the kitchen, because cooking is just as creative and imaginative an activity as drawing, or wood carving, or music."

-Julia Child

78

Turn your palate into your palette.

The world of dining and cooking holds its own creative magic, with pots and pans as artist's palettes, and the plate as the canvas. Delve into the culinary universe and use the world of sauces, spices, barbeque, or cake decorating as your exploratory domain.

79

Picture your own restaurant.

This is an exercise in delicious visualization. If you owned your own, beautiful restaurant, what style of food would you serve? What would be your famous-across-the-land specialty? What would the décor be like? Who would be your customers? Would you have live music, cooking classes, or other happenings at your place?

80

Design a sample menu—just for fun.

Whether or not you actually start your own restaurant or café business, planning out the dream can still do wonders for stirring your passion—and honing your skills—for creative endeavors. Designing a menu for a restaurant or café is a prime avenue for brainstorming, as you merge your entrepreneurial spirit with strategic vision and vivid imagination.

81

Explore the wide world of wine.

Attend a wine tasting and discover new facts about the featured wines, their regions and their winemakers. Does one particular wine or region stand out for you? Research, taste, and learn more about this wine, and create a theme night around it with someone special. Accompany your honored wine with dinner and a movie, event, or a good book, all relating to a common theme.

For example, if you enjoy Chianti Classico wine (from Italy's Tuscany region), enjoy a juicy *Bistecca alla Fiorentina* and watch a movie such as *Under the Tuscan Sun* or *A Room With a View*. Get creative with your themes—the more inventive, the more fun!

82

Get to know classic

food and wine pairings.

Study—and then sample—a variety of food and wine combinations. Keep a journal as to what works for you and what doesn't. Well-known pairings have become classics for a reason. Some are so delicious, they've been described as transcendental! One such classic pairing is English Stilton cheese with vintage port.

83

Experiment with your own

food and wine combinations.

Once you've sampled the classics, it's time to experiment with new combinations and test your palate. What is the most unusual combination you can think of? Be bold. Be open. You might surprise yourself. Champagne and potato chips, anyone?

84

Start a culinary collection.

Gathering and collecting things we love can bring us back to our childhoods, becoming absorbed and engaged for hours in our own world. While this approach works for just about any collectible, there are many opportunities for collecting things in the culinary arena.

My aunt has been collecting unusual salt and pepper shakers for decades. What floats your boat? Do you enjoy wines from around the world? Various types of mustards or jellies? Exotic spices for your spice rack? How about cookbooks? Once you get started, you may discover your appetite for collecting is insatiable.

85

Visit ethnic markets around town.

Imagine having a sampling of the world in your own city. Demographically, this may be true, depending on where you live. But even more likely, your city has several different types of ethnic markets around town, carrying specialty items that are popular in their countries of origin. Be adventurous! Browse in these shops, see what piques your interest, and bring home a new item to incorporate into your cooking this week.

86

Add a blindfold to your meal.

It is said that when one sense is muted, our other senses become sharpened. Get together with a "foodie" friend or lover and create a literal "blind tasting" of an elaborate meal. Make a game out of it, by having your partner guess the food while blindfolded, or by tasting a food in different forms to savor the nuances.

87

Orchestrate a meal by flavors or textures.

Whether through contrasts or similarities, meals that focus on the texture of foods are an exercise in both the mind and the senses. This is what the great chefs do, so why not try this at home? Think about which foods would go best together. How about a complementary meal of rich, robust foods? Or a contrasting experience: When one food is crispy, its counterpart is creamy. Sprinkle a surprising garnish on a dish. Or tease your tongue with a sweet and spicy combo. (Just like in tip #86, you can step this up with a blindfold!)

CONFETTI REFLECTION

When it comes to **gourmet pursuits,** what are some unique ways that you express your passions and creativity? What new ideas can you explore in this area? Use the spaces below to jot down your thoughts.

1._____

_____

2._____

_____

3._____

_____

4._____

_____

5._____

Religion and Spirituality

*"Faith is the highest passion
in a human being."*

-Søren Kierkegaard

88

Revisit your place of worship.

Have you been to your house of worship recently? If you do attend a church, synagogue, temple or other house of prayer, but haven't been there in a while, revisit your congregation's services for a dose of faith and camaraderie. While you've been away, you have grown and evolved. You may discover new meanings in old traditions.

89

Meditate on an uplifting idea.

For some, organized religion is not the only route to spiritual connection. Calm your mind and think about the universe around you, and your role and purpose in it. Who are you? What do you believe your purpose is in this life? How can you help and love your fellow humankind?

These are significant questions to ponder—and you may have different questions yourself—but there are many resources to assist you on this journey, such as the spiritual programs of Abraham-Hicks Publications (Abraham-Hicks.com).

90

Create a vision board.

There is a metaphysical belief that our thoughts become things, manifested into our physical world and into our own life experiences. The good news about this concept is that we control our thoughts—so therefore, we can control what comes forth from them. Visualization is a key enhancer of our thoughts, so why not create a vision board depicting positive realities, like your ideal lifestyle and achievements?

Create a collage of words, quotes, and images that excite and inspire you. Display your vision board in a prominent place. You can even create a digital version through graphics software, or websites like DigitalDreamBoard.com

91

Revisit your vision board daily.

Pay attention to your vision board. Look at it often, and envision your desired goals and lifestyle in vivid detail, as if you are already living them. What does your ideal life look like? How do you spend your day? With whom? Where do you live? Feel the passion and the energy that emanate from the idea of having all that you desire. There is power in these types of thoughts, as they are believed to be linked to universal vibrations of manifestation.

92

Practice gratitude.

Think about your life. Your health, your family, your job, your friends, your natural talents, your good heart—and so many other things!—that make your experiences what they are. From having food on the table to having opportunities for education and growth, there is much to be thankful for every day. Practice gratitude and appreciation for all that you have, and all that you are.

The emotion behind gratitude invites the universe to respond in kind, with more reasons to be grateful appearing all the time. You may also want to start a gratitude journal, and to write in it each day before bed or first thing in the morning.

CONFETTI REFLECTION

When it comes to **religion and spirituality**, what are some unique ways that you express your passions and creativity? What new ideas can you explore in this area? Use the spaces below to jot down your thoughts.

1._____

_____

2._____

_____

3._____

_____

4._____

_____

5._____

Health and Wellness

"Health is a state of complete physical, mental and social well-being, and not merely the absence of disease or infirmity."

- World Health Organization

93

Eat well, and (literally) feed your passions.

Eat healthy, wholesome foods, but do not force yourself to eat things you do not like. Chances are, if you truly listen to your body (and not just to your taste buds), you will reach for what you need to feel nourished. Forget about "waistline" thinking, and think about feeding your brain, your creative garden!

94

Get enough sleep.

Creativity is exhilarating, and passion is joyous, but these fully-engaging experiences can be physically draining on the body. Make sure you allow yourself enough time to fully recharge every night. Resist temptations like zoning out to late-night TV or Internet surfing, which can be addictive and can cut into valuable sleep time. Be sure that your sleeping area reflects a peaceful tone. Try to keep work documents, bills, and other stressful reminders out of the bedroom.

95

Take a power nap.

If your schedule allows it, enjoy a power nap. Turn off all electronic devices like phones and televisions, and darken the room. To help get into an instant mode of relaxation, imagine that you've just slipped back into bed after pressing the "snooze" button on your alarm—savor every last minute you are curled up under the covers! If kept to less than 30 minutes, this impromptu rest period should give you renewed pep, clarity and focus for the rest of the day.

96

Check in with your doctor.

Stay on top of your regular check-ups with your doctor. Good health plays an important role in the ability to enjoy our passions fully, and to freely follow our creative inspirations. Knowing the status of your health is a sign of respecting your body. If there is something to fix, it is better to know about it; and if all is healthy, then that peace of mind is a true gift.

97

Get moving with an activity

you actually enjoy.

Nothing kills the passionate spirit faster than sweating it out with a sour face, feeling that we are exercising "because we have to." There is likely an activity that you would genuinely enjoy, that would give you physical benefits, as well. Think dancing, tennis, kickboxing, hiking, skiing, swimming, racquetball, biking, hip-hop….think outside the treadmill!

98

Add music to your day.

This goes beyond the usual customs of exercising to music, or attending a music concert. If you play your favorite tunes as a backdrop to your daily activities, from driving to cleaning, you will find that the added musical pep adds a spring to your step—and boosts your creative flow in other areas of your life. Besides, it is far better to have a song stuck in your head than a constant playback of stressful thoughts.

99

Nurture through nature.

Think lush…calm…peaceful…green… abundant… Spend some time in nature. Whether you prefer vigorous activities, like hiking and biking, or meandering through shady gardens, get out among the trees, the blooms of the season, and the fresh air. Have a picnic near a stream or make a point to catch a beautiful sunset. Take a cue from the Japanese: Create your own rock garden and rake the pebbles into designs while you meditate on the task.

100

Give yourself some breathing room.

Schedule enough downtime to allow your creative spirit to breathe. The paradox of being highly creative and having many passions is that our tendency is to want to do it all, and do it now. Saying "yes" to life is exhilarating, but it can also be exhausting! Beware any "Type A" tendencies to guzzle from the stream of life and flutter around in non-stop achievement mode. Make sure you are leaving enough open spaces in your schedule to recharge and avoid burn-out. This is actually a key to fresh and prolonged creativity.

101

Bolster your support network.

It all goes back to the people in our lives. Whether it is your family, a close-knit network of friends, or a reliable partner, having a circle of people who genuinely care about you is the way to bring love, and therefore joy, and therefore creativity and passion, into your life.

CONFETTI REFLECTION

When it comes to **health and wellness,** what are some unique ways that you express your passions and creativity? What new ideas can you explore in this area? Use the spaces below to jot down your thoughts.

1._____

_____

2._____

_____

3._____

_____

4._____

_____

5._____

Your Own Confetti Path

Dear reader,

Thank you for joining me on this colorful journey of creative themes and variations. Now, let's hear from you!

What did you discover through THE CONFETTI PATH? Do you have your own special tips for enhancing creativity and passion that were not listed here?

I would love to hear your personal stories, feedback, and comments about your own approach to creative and passionate living. Please feel free to share your thoughts with me, at **info@ConfettiPath.com**

May you follow your muse, always.

-G.B.

About the Author

Gilat Ben-Dor, MBA, CSW is an author, speaker, and the founder of GUSTO POWER®, a personal and professional development program that helps Multi-Passionate Professionals™ successfully manage their many talents. A creative "multipreneur" herself, Gilat has created several successful businesses, including a wine academy, a publishing company, and an online emporium featuring Gilat's art and photography. Gilat is also an adjunct faculty member at a nationally recognized university. She holds an MBA in Global Management and lives in Scottsdale, Arizona.

For more information about Gilat Ben-Dor, visit her central web site, **GilatBen-Dor.com**

To learn more about Gilat Ben-Dor's GUSTO POWER® success program, visit **GustoPower.com**

For THE CONFETTI PATH's official book website, visit **ConfettiPath.com**

Additional Opportunities

Speaking, Coaching,

Consulting and Workshops

with Gilat Ben-Dor

Imagine sharing your insights and inspirations from THE CONFETTI PATH with your organization and your network. Dynamic speaker, author, coach and consultant Gilat Ben-Dor is passionate about bringing more creativity, productivity, and peace of mind to Multi-Passionate Professionals™ and their teams.

For more information about booking Gilat Ben-Dor for your organization, please email info@GustoPower.com

Gilat Ben-Dor's presentation formats include keynote and conference speaking, break-out sessions, workshops/seminars, webinars, consulting, and Platinum one-on-one coaching. Suggested audiences include:

- Leaders & Managers
- Creative Professionals
- Associations
- Entrepreneurs
- Universities

As a complement to the message of her book, THE CONFETTI PATH: 101 Ways to Celebrate Your Passions and Inspire Creativity, Gilat Ben-Dor offers a special presentation:

Finding Your Confetti Path:
The Colorful Road to Everyday Inspiration™

Filled with opportunities for group participation and engaging activity, this empowering, idea-sparking presentation can be adapted to either a workshop or a traditional keynote speaking format. Both business and personal-growth groups, including creative professionals, can benefit from this message of looking beyond the concrete road in front of us, and coming away with a new path of colorful nuggets! (Also suitable for college and high-school audiences)

Some of Gilat Ben-Dor's additional presentation topics include:

GUSTO POWER®: Power Skills for the Multi-Passionate Professional™

Gilat's signature keynote of the Gusto Power® program, this presentation is ideal for both corporate and entrepreneurial groups. Through engaging stories, humor and pertinent case studies, the audience will take away a new understanding of the benefits of exploring our diverse sets of talents. Participants will learn simple, effective "Power Skills" they can apply immediately to increase personal satisfaction, workplace morale, and professional productivity.

Like a Diamond: The Brilliance and Benefits of Multi-Faceted Careers™

Many of us have been conditioned to believe that professionally, we must only do one thing and be one thing. But this shoe does not fit everyone, and holding back can short-change both ourselves and our organizations. This eye-opening presentation will reveal the untapped potential — and how to unleash it — from each individual, and how this immense pool of hidden talents can result in profitable partnerships and synergies.

Creative Nine-to-Five: Branching Out While Punching In™

Although specialists have traditionally been valued, the definition of a valued employee is rapidly changing. With economic shakedowns and a new corporate landscape, today's MVE (Most Valuable Employee) can do more by calling upon all sides of themselves. This keynote combines case studies, personal experiences, and an uplifting message that celebrates the value employees offer their organization by being multi-faceted professionals.

Book discounts available for bulk purchases. For details,
please inquire with the publisher: info@GilatMedia.com

GUSTO P9WER™

Notes

Notes

Notes

Notes